GARDENING WITH
PETER DOWDALL

First published in 2010 by Atrium
Atrium is an imprint of Cork University Press
Youngline Industrial Estate, Pouladuff Road, Togher, Cork, Ireland

British Library Cataloguing in Publication Data

A CIP catalogue record for this book is available from the British Library.

ISBN 978-1855942-15-8

Book design and typesetting: Anú Design, Tara
Printed in Navarra, Spain by Graphy Cems

For all Atrium books visit www.corkuniversitypress.com

GARDENING WITH
PETER DOWDALL

The Importance of the Natural World

ATRIUM

To the two people without whom
there would be no garden,
my parents, Finbarr and Rosemary

Contents

Magnolia

Introduction

This is a no-nonsense guide to gardening. Being a no-nonsense gardener myself, what I wanted most was to provide an easy-to-use guide for the beginner gardener on how to build and maintain a beautiful garden. And through these pages I hope to offer a greater understanding of the part that gardening and nature plays in our day-to-day lives, in our health, and in our general well-being.

My love for gardening stretches back as far as I can remember. As a toddler, I wandered around the garden with my mother, watching her take cuttings and helping her to plant them. I sowed seeds and filled beds and pots with plants that just weeks later would be a blaze of colour. If, as a three-year-old, I could get plants to grow, then surely there can be no mystery to it. That is what I try to instil in people. Don't be scared of the garden – give it a go. Don't be put off by all the technical terms and the Latin names, just remember how simple it is: you put a plant or a seed in the ground and it grows – after that, it's all just extras. If I can impart a love for gardening to just one reader, then this book will have been a success.

A five-year battle with cancer in my twenties gave me an entirely new outlook on life and living and the vital link between me and the natural world around me. It was nature that helped me to heal – from the tree that I could see through my hospital room window, which taught me to appreciate each passing season, to the herbs that naturally eased my discomfort, to the overwhelming desire to get back outside and work with plants in their natural setting. I kept a journal during my illness, both when I first developed cancer in 1994 and when I relapsed in 1997. Each chapter here is introduced with an excerpt from that journal and a reflection that links my life, and my way of thinking about life and nature, with the themes of this book.

Hydrangea

the Naked Garden

When embarking on your first garden, or starting a new year of planting, there are a few questions you should ask yourself. Why do you want a garden? What do you want from it? Do you want a manicured cutting green, or are you more the type of person who wants a wildflower meadow in the heart of the city? Maybe you want to do nothing but grow vegetables and make compost.

1

Trees outside my bedroom window delight me and infuriate me. In particular, a beautiful lime tree is situated on the lower level of the grounds of the hospital overlooking the river. It is the shape of this tree that makes it so dramatically stunning. Watching it come into leaf in April is enthralling. It gives me pleasure to admire it, but it is also a torture to see the summer starting and the natural world coming back into growth. I love watching the spring breathe vibrancy into the seemingly dormant landscape, but it also acts a reminder that time is marching on . . .

I knew this tree of old. A lovely specimen, I had first met this *Tilia* in December 1994 and had watched it get dressed in the spring of 1995. I underwent treatment right through that year until September, and watched it undress again that winter when I was readmitted for check-up scans. I loved the tree but really did not want to see it again from my hospital window. I would have much rather have got to know it at closer quarters.

When I went back into hospital in September 1997, this same tree was just beginning to lose its leaves, and I calculated its cycle like a timing device. I was in hospital for tests, I told myself; they would find out what was wrong with me, and by the time the winter had finished its work and the tree had

come back into leaf the following spring, I would be better.

But, as it happened, I was not finished with the hospital by the time its leaves started to appear in the spring of 1998. The horror was only just beginning again. Even by the time the cruel winter of that year had stripped my *Tilia* bare, I seemed to be no closer to the end of the road.

Seasons were moving on and I was watching all this happen from inside room 401. I was acutely aware that

Figure 1
A naked garden space.

The all-knowing, all-seeing lime tree in the grounds of the Bons Secours hospital, Cork, a tree with whom I developed a love/hate relationship.

these years would not be given to me again. And I began to resent the tree. It stood there in all its majesty. It had nothing to worry about. It did not have to worry about being sick. It did not have to worry about getting better. It did not have the ability to worry at all. It did not have to suffer the horrors of chemotherapy, nor did it have to fret about when it would next be in for treatment. It just stood there simply doing its thing. It did not care whether I lived or died. It was there before I was ever on this earth and it would be there long after I departed it. It would go on producing leaves and dropping leaves, oblivious to my suffering and the suffering of every soul who looked upon it day after day from the same hospital windows, oblivious to my very existence. Or was it?

First Things First

When embarking on your first garden, or starting a new year of planting, there are a few questions you should ask yourself. Why do you want a garden? What do you want from it? Do you want a manicured putting green, or are you more the type of person who wants a wildflower meadow in the heart of the city? Maybe you want to do nothing but grow vegetables and make compost. Or perhaps you want a combination of all of these things, and a place for the kids to play. Now,

more than ever before, the garden should be looked at as an 'outdoor room'. As we are spending more time in our homes for work, leisure and entertaining, it makes sense to put some time and effort into your garden. It is often the biggest room of the house and decorating it can give such pleasure and provide a unique opportunity to express yourself. But where do you start? Literally thousands of varieties of plants are available for purchase, and starting out on the journey of creating your garden can seem a daunting task. The incredible choice of flowers alone, so many flowers, not to mention the myriad Latin names and technical terms associated with gardening, can be bewildering to a beginner.

But first things first. Like most projects, research and preparation are fundamental – it is important not to put the wrong plant in the wrong place, and I will show you how to pick the right plants for your individual situation.

Once you have decided on the kind of outdoor room you want for your home, you can begin the process of building the space. As with any extension to your house, you must first start with the structural components. And the biggest structural components in any garden are the trees and shrubs that provide natural 'walls' and borders. We will begin your garden there . . .

Trees

It is easy to have a garden looking well in summer with flowers in full bloom, but the art of good garden planning is to create a garden that looks well in all four seasons. Winter is the time for designing, planning and constructing a new garden. It is a good time to plant, because the plants get the chance to get established before actively growing in the spring. Also, wintertime allows you to see the skeleton of your garden, as many plants are leafless and your eye is not being distracted with a colourful array of foliage and flowers. If you get the skeleton of the garden correct, you are well on the road to creating a good garden. I don't want to use the phrase 'perfect garden', because I don't like the thought of a perfect garden.

Keeping all this in mind, you must first decide upon a choice of tree, or trees, and architectural plants. If your garden is big enough to take one tree, or even more than one, then you are lucky, because trees are one of nature's greatest gifts. They act as huge environmental mops, cleaning up air pollutants such as carbon monoxide, and capturing carbon dioxide, the most important of the greenhouse gases, which is absorbed and stored

Trees planted this close to a house obstruct air and light from getting to the house.

by trees. And trees produce oxygen – in one season alone, a mature tree will produce more oxygen than ten people will inhale in a year. From a less scientific but equally important point of view, trees act as great sound barriers; they will protect the garden from wind damage and, of course, provide beautiful shade on the long, balmy summer days. And remember, trees are there for us to admire and enjoy but they also provide places of refuge and food sources for a myriad of wildlife. Trees can be homes and drive-in restaurants for these little guys.

Which tree to go for, then? You need to bear in mind a couple of physical factors when choosing the right tree for your garden. Consider the distances between the tree's position in your garden and the house and other structures: you want to avoid any damage the tree may cause in a storm. When you are considering this, it is important to know ultimate height and spread of the tree when it reaches maturity. Remember that the roots of most trees will be as wide as their crowns, so regard the outermost branches and leaves and then look straight down from there and that is where the roots will be. And check if the roots will be interfering with sewerage pipes or septic tanks,

Not only is this tree planted far too close to the house but it is also creating too much shade over the whole garden area.

or even the foundations of the house.

Bearing these factors in mind, you are now ready to choose the best tree for your garden from a horticultural point of view. Where do you want to plant your tree? This is hugely important, as trees are the most imposing feature in any garden. They will command attention all year round: from the naked branches in the winter to the burgeoning new growth in the spring, through the bountiful leaves, flowers and seed production in the summer, to the outstanding colour that is produced during the autumn as the leaves enter their old age and go out in all their fiery-coloured glory.

Trees will create shade, so think where you would like that shady area to be. Do you want the tree to block out the sun? Probably not!

Trees are going to be the feature that the whole garden works around, so don't plant them independently of the rest of the garden, they should be worked into your overall plan.

The best part of the process is deciding on the trees that you want to plant. This will involve countless reference books, trips online, visits to garden centres and gardens open to the public. For a large garden, I suggest the following: Horse chestnut (*Aesculus hippocastanum*), common beech (*Fagus sylvatica*), and common oak (*Quercus robur*).

Horse Chestnut
(Aesculus hippocastanum)
This Irish favourite is actually native to south-eastern Europe and western Asia. In spring or early summer the palmate leaves appear, and in May the horse chestnut lights up with large white, candle-like flowers, spotted yellow and pinky red. This tree has been chosen to decorate parklands all over Europe. Spiny fruit appear in late June and ripen in September, falling in October, when children collect the chestnuts, or conkers, to play their favourite autumn game. Deer also eat the nuts.

Height: 15–30 m **Spread:** 15–20 m.
Aspect: Grow in full sun.
Soil type: prefers a soil that is moist but well-drained; but fairly soil adaptable.
Flowers: May to June.
Pests: Pests are not normally a problem with this tree; however, horse chestnuts in the UK are suffering increased levels of attack from the horse chestnut leaf miner and from a fungal pathogen commonly known as bleeding canker.
Medicinal uses: horse chestnut seeds are toxic; however, they contain the chemical saponin known as aescin, which in clinical studies has been reported to promote increased blood circulation. It is also thought that aescin may possess anti-inflammatory properties useful in reducing oedema, swelling caused by excess fluid, as a result of injury. Poultices of the seed have been used to treat skin ulcers and skin cancer; however, **there is no evidence to validate its effectiveness.**

Sunlight breaking through the distinctive leaves of the Horse Chestnut, *Aesculus hippocastanum*.

7

Common Beech
(Fagus sylvatica)

Beech trees are attractive throughout the year. In early spring their red, pointed buds open to reveal bright green leaves, which darken through May, June and July. Beech trees can reach a spread of 30 m and are usually taller than their spread. The leaves are a lovely sight in springtime, as they change through many shades of green. The purple form, *Atropurpurea*, or the copper beech, has purple leaves and is a sight to behold during the spring as the buds are bursting into leaf. In April and May the flowers appear, and in autumn fruits, known as beech mast, ripen and burst to reveal three brown nuts within each husk. Beech is tolerant of a wide range of soil conditions, including well-drained chalk. On heavy clay, however, hornbeam (*Carpinus betulus*) is a better choice.

Beech can also be grown as a beautiful hedge. It is slow growing and can be kept at any height over 1 m. Although a deciduous hedge, it does not drop its leaves during the winter. The leaves turn brown and die but remain on the hedge until new leaves appearing in the spring push them off. This creates a wonderful chocolate brown effect on the hedge during the winter months.

Height: 15–40 m / Spread: 15–30 m.
Aspect: Grow in full sun to partial shade.
Soil type: performs best in deep, rich, evenly moist, well-drained, slightly acidic soils. Needs to be well watered in the first year.
Flowers: April to May.
Pests: Beech is not affected by many pests; however, the fungus *Meripilus giganteus*, the giant polypore, is a common cause of death in mature beech trees. A hard fungal growth around the tree's base and a lot of dieback in the stems indicate the presence of an attack, although the tree will often look in perfect health otherwise.

One of the monarchs of the tree world, a copse of beech in all their glory (left).

Common Oak
(Quercus robur)

The national tree of Ireland, the majestic oak is noted for its vigorous, luxuriant growth. *Quercus robur* grows very quickly to a height of 20 m tall with a spread of up to 20 m and a low-branching canopy. Few sights are as impressive as a mature specimen oak tree. The autumn foliage is a rich dark brown. Oak grows best in free-draining soils, but will tolerate many soil types. In ideal sites it will grow at least 1 m per year, and will become a grand tree within two decades.

Height: 25 m / **Spread:** 25 m over fifty years.
Aspect: Grow in full sun or partial shade.
Soil type: must be deep and well-drained.
Flowers: May to June.
Pests: leaf mining moths, aphids, caterpillars and oak gall wasps.
Diseases: mainly oak galls and powdery mildew.

The most majestic of them all, *Quercus robur* (Oak).

These three trees will grow into huge specimens, though never will the person who plants them get to see them in maturity, as they can live for several hundred years.

For smaller gardens there are countless trees that will create the architectural effect you are after, as well as producing flowers, attractive bark and stems and providing food sources for birds and other creatures. Some of the best for colour and contrast are: mountain ash/rowan (*Sorbus aucuparia*); whitebeam (*Sorbus aria* 'Lutescens'); Midland hawthorn (*Crataegus laevigata* 'Paul's Scarlet'); and my favourite of all the smaller trees, Himalayan birch (*Betula utilis* var. *jacquemontii*).

The beautiful red autumn colour and winter berries of the mountain ash.

Mountain Ash/Rowan
(Sorbus aucuparia)

Mountain ash foliage emerges afresh each spring to clothe the tree in dark green compound leaves, composed of 7 to 13 sharply toothed leaflets. It has a grey-brown, smooth and shiny bark. From May to June, the tree produces its summer clusters of creamy-white blooms, which on mature specimens can contain up to 250 flowers per cluster. The leaves provide excellent autumn colour of orange, red and brown. September to October is when the bright red berries (8 mm wide) are at their peak, providing a valuable food source for the many woodland garden inhabitants, including thrushes and blackbirds.

Height: 5–6 m / **Spread:** 2–3 m.
Aspect: Grow in full sun or light shade.
Soil type: tolerant of most soils but prefers a slightly acidic soil.
Pests: aphids and sawflies.
Diseases: canker and, much more rarely, fireblight and silver leaf.

The red flowers of
Crataeagus laevigata
'Pauls Scarlet' (right).

Whitebeam
(*Sorbus aria* 'Lutescens')

This very striking tree is at its finest in early spring when its leaves are bursting out of the buds. Every day during this period the tree changes colour slightly, from a very delicate, fresh spring green to a silver-green in late summer. Clusters of white flowers appear in early summer, followed by red fruits in autumn. The bark of the tree has beige and orange tones, with beautiful variations. It makes a good attractive specimen tree, which is fairly wind resistant.

Height: 5 m **Spread:** 3 m.
Aspect: Grow in full sun or partial shade.
Soil type: most soils.
Pests: not affected by many pests; aphids can do a certain amount of damage.

Himalayan Birch
(*Betula utilis* var. *jacquemontii*)

The magnificent Himalayan birch will brighten any garden all year round. Many silver-stemmed birches are available but this one is possibly the most dramatic and most commonly available of the silver birches. It has a pure white bark, which improves with age, and medium-sized, heart-shaped leaves. This attractive tree has beautifully textured stems, a lovely shape, wonderful buttery-yellow autumnal colouring and in winter the peeling bark reveals intense, fresh, milky-white limbs. You must resist the temptation to peel the bark, as this will damage the tree. The small, oval-toothed leaves show dark green, before taking on the autumnal hues and dropping.

Height: 6 m **Spread:** 2–3 m.
Aspect: Grow in full sun or partial shade.
Soil type: most soils, including well-drained /light, clay/heavy, acidic, moist, sandy.
Pests: some damage from aphids; otherwise not known to suffer much from pest damage.

Betula utilis var. jacquemontii showing fantastic autumn colour.

Midland Hawthorn
(*Crataegus laevigata* 'Paul's Scarlet')

This lovely tree, commonly known as the double red hawthorn, is one of the finest for spring and autumn display. Midland hawthorn is ideal for wildlife-friendly gardens, where its dense, thorny cover makes it suitable for hedging and provides good nesting sites for a whole range of small birds. In April and May it produces red flowers and it has attractive, glossy, dark green leaves. In autumn a display of deep red berries provides bright colour and a source of winter food for resident birds and winter visitors. A very good tree for urban areas, as it can tolerate pollution and act as a refuge for wildlife.

Height: 5 m **Spread:** 2 m.
Aspect: Grow in full sun or partial shade.
Soil type: will grow well in nearly all soils.
Flowers: May to June.
Pests: resistant to most pests.

Planting Trees

A tree may be planted for aesthetic reasons, or in the cause of environmental sustainability, or even just to satisfy the desire for a swing. Whatever the reason, everyone should be encouraged to plant one.

When you are planting a tree, keep these things in mind:

- Choose a healthy specimen: there should be no signs of pest or disease damage.

- If you are planting a bare root tree (a tree that has been lifted from the ground and has not been grown in a pot), only do so from November to February. At all other times of the year use potted trees.

- Dig a hole big enough to accommodate the roots of the tree and some organic matter, such as well-rotted farmyard manure and compost.

- Stake the tree properly. This timber stake is not for decoration, it can make the difference between the tree developing properly and thus thriving or not. The purpose of staking is to make sure that the tree is well anchored into the soil. The roots of the tree must not be allowed to rock in the soil. Position the stake in line with the prevailing wind and tie the tree to the stake twice – at about 50 cm and 150 cm from the ground – ensuring that the tree is not rubbing against the stake at any point.

- If rabbits are a problem, or even if you think that they might be in the area, put a rabbit guard around the base of the tree.

- Before you can sit back and enjoy the tree maturing, you have one more job to do – you must water it. During the first growing season, the roots of the newly planted tree will be unable to get enough water from the soil, as they will not have developed sufficiently, so it is essential that you provide the tree with regular watering.

Architectural Plants

When you are preparing your garden, keep in mind that architectural plants don't have to be big trees, they just need to be plants with a definite structure and point of interest. Ornamental grasses and grass type plants can be very architectural, offering definite shape, texture and, often, movement to a garden. Some of my favourites are *Stipa*, *Miscanthus* and *Pennisetum*, each genus having many species and cultivars. One of the loveliest is *Stipa gigantea*, or giant oat grass as it is commonly known, which can reach a height of 2.5 m in one year.

This grass makes a bold statement during the summer, producing beautiful airy flowers on top of tall stems. It will create a commanding presence wherever it is planted. In the winter, *S. gigantea* will die back dramatically.

Stipa tenuissima 'Pony Tails' is an equally attractive, but very different, grass. It will grow to about 90 cm in height and a mature plant will form a clump about 1.5 m in width. It is thicker and more dense than *S. gigantea* but is still very graceful and elegant.

Stipa arundinacea, or pheasant's tail grass, will grow to about 1 m in height and about the same in width. You can plant it and admire its elegance and form all summer long, but it is when the days shorten and autumn approaches that this plant comes into its own, showing beautiful orange/red/green hues.

Miscanthus sinensis 'Klien Fontaine', 'Gracillimus' and 'Silberfeder' to mention just three cultivars, are also grasses that really perform during the autumn. In the spring they awake from their winter sleep and send forth shoots, which in summer will produce flowers that by autumn have begun to take on the appearance of cotton wool on stems. But it is the fantastic leaf and stem colour that make these plants

Stipa gigantea adds movement and form to any garden planting (top); *Stipa* 'Pony Tails' (bottom), one of the nicest of all for texture. You simply cannot walk past it without wanting to touch it.

The flowers and later the seed heads of this *Miscanthus* provide a valuable food source for birds in the garden and the structure of the plant adds a real feeling of movement to the garden.

worthy of mention and essential choices for the garden.

One of the best grasses for flowering in the garden is *Pennisetum*.

Fantastic plumes of flowers are produced on delicate arching stems. A plant in full flower viewed from a distance can appear like candyfloss. Try the dwarf variety *Pennisetum alopecuroides* 'Hameln', which grows to about 30 cm.

I have left the best feature of all these grasses to last – their exquisite movement. The gentle sway of these beautiful grasses is possibly their finest feature architecturally. They dance away happily even in the faintest of breezes and you can almost feel their discomfort when storms and gales flatten them to the earth.

Grasses are only one type of architectural plant that can give structure to your garden, but they perfectly illustrate what I mean by plants that create structure and an architectural point in the garden.

You need to remember that gardening is not collecting. The person with the most plants does not win. A good garden needs to have a bit of structure, even if it is not immediately apparent. What a good garden also needs is a bit of space in its design so that the structure can be seen.

Two extremes in design can be best summed up with images. At one end of the scale, there are the very structural, symmetrical and formal

Pennisetums like this one are grown for their very attractive flower heads (left). This garden (bottom) appears very structured and formal due to the use of box hedging to create different planting areas, and also the fact that nothing is growing out of place.

The informal but very attractive cottage garden.

gardens such as the knot gardens of old and the gardens of the chateaux in France.

At the other end, you have the delightfully informal English cottage garden effect.

The former style is very rigid, exact and structural, and the latter gives the effect of complete nonchalance, as if everything happened by accident. But things rarely happen by accident. In a good informal garden there will always be some structure and care given to the planting.

There is a fine line between having too much structure and none at all, but I am certainly not the one to make any rules as to what is too little and what is too much in your garden. Gardening is supposed to be an individual pursuit. By all means read the rules and guidelines, but if you want my advice, after you have read them, throw them out. It is important to understand the basic general principles of design, but once you have a grasp of them, your specific garden design should be 100 per cent up to you.

An architectural plant does not have to be a dramatic, large tree. It is simply something that creates a focal point and ideally it should be valuable to the garden each month of the year. That does not mean that it needs to be evergreen, however. Some evergreen plants and conifers can be the least structural of all plants, while deciduous plants, such as *Corylus avellana* 'Contorta' (corkscrew hazel), commands your attention with its dramatically twisted stems and catkins throughout the entire year.

The twisted stem of the corkscrew hazel are a dramatic addition to the winter garden.

Beschorneria yuccoides 'Quicksilver', not only has a real mouthful of a name, it is also an incredibly dramatic structural plant.

These are plants that you will work other plants and features around. And, remember, one of the best ways of creating a structure or balance in the garden is by repeated use of the same architectural plant.

Beschorneria yuccoides Quicksilver.

After all, this will be your space and it should have your stamp on it. In the same way as there are many different styles of painting, so too are there numerous styles of gardening. If you are very ordered and structured in your life, then maybe your garden will also be very structured, or maybe this is where you will let loose. It can be great fun to be like Eliot's J. Alfred Prufrock when you are in the garden and 'wear the bottoms of my trousers rolled'. In other words, the garden is a place where you don't have to conform to society's rules and regulations; you are free to be yourself and to express yourself. If you are anything like me, a bit all over the place and certainly not structured, then your garden will be a bit of a mixture.

This 'careless' structure can be achieved by using the same architectural plant in a few different positions in the garden. It really can be as simple as that. This planting technique can tie together a mixture of plants and planting to create a subtle sense of order that, while creatively chaotic, will not confuse the eye. So it is also a good idea to give some thought, not only to where you position the architectural plants, but also to the combinations of architectural plants you wish to use and which other plants will work best with them. Again, repetition of combinations will provide structure to the garden.

Pruning grasses like this is best done just before the growth starts in the spring.

A Rough Guide to Pruning

Grasses

Many ornamental grasses are herbaceous, in other words they will die back completely for the winter. All you need to do when they die back is remove the dead growth over the ground for cleanliness. However, some herbaceous grasses such as the *Miscanthus* create a dramatic winter garden effect with frost on the dead stems and seed heads, which also provide a food source for birds during these harsh months. Most evergreen grasses will benefit from a haircut in early to mid spring. Grab them tightly in your hand or tie them up with some twine and cut them back by as much as 60 per cent to tidy them up. This will remove much of the untidy growth and also promote clean, new growth as the temperatures increase.

This evergreen *Magnolia* may take a number of years to flower but it is worth it.

Cytisus will do well in a limey soil and produce masses of flower in spring and early summer.

Pink *Hydrangeas* like this one will retain their pink colour on limey soils.

Red Admiral butterfly enjoying the beautiful *Hebe*.

Hebe

Photinia x fraseri 'Red Robin'

Green is More than a Colour

In a country that is famed for its many shades of green, it is important to keep evergreens in mind when you are building your garden. Once you have decided on your tree, or trees, it is time to start considering other plants. Where do you begin? Well, every garden needs a certain number of evergreen plants for structure and interest and also to provide refuge for wildlife during the winter.

2

A garden with too
much evergreen
planting can be dull as
it offers no seasonal
interest and changes
(right); A garden can
look very bare and
bleak in the winter if
not planted correctly
(below).

These plants, along with the
structural trees and architectural plants,
are going to form the real crux of the
garden, so it is important that you
make the right choices for your own
individual outdoor room. If after a
few years you feel that your choice of
evergreens was not right, then it will
be quite a job to remove and replace
them. For if you decide to change
your evergreens, you will in essence
be removing some of the garden's
maturity and have to start again
from scratch.

On the flip side, though, a garden that is full of evergreen plants, to the exclusion of everything else, can be the dullest garden in the world.

All too often we can get hung up on wanting our plants to have foliage all year round. By creating this type of garden, we are missing all the seasonal changes that bring a garden to life. On the other hand, a garden that is completely deciduous and herbaceous, and thus bare in the winter, is also not the right way to go.

Balance is the gardener's buzzword. You need a combination of plants to keep interest in the garden each month of the year.

Evergreens can create natural borders, either sectioning off one part of your garden from the next, or separating your neighbour's garden from your own.

Some areas will even demand evergreen plants – perhaps there is an unsightly oil tank or outbuilding that needs to be screened, or maybe you

This beech hedge (below) is used to divide the garden in two, forcing you to look to see what is behind and dividing a garden into a series of 'rooms'.

want to keep your well-managed composting area from view. In those situations, or when you want plants to provide you with some privacy from neighbouring windows and gardens, evergreens are a must.

A mixture of both evergreen and deciduous plants can also work. One good combination, which will work as a tall screen to create privacy, is *Prunus cerasifera* 'Nigra' (cherry plum) and *Thuja occidentalis* 'Smaragd' (white cedar). The *Prunus* produces beautiful, pale pink flowers on naked branches from February to early April,

prior to the arrival of the tree's rich purple foliage, which remains until late October. The *Thuja* stands proud, a stately conifer growing to about 4–5 m in height, with a spread of 1–1.5 m. I like this conifer because it is not a bully, like so many of them can be. It is a neat evergreen plant that requires no pruning and virtually no maintenance.

An equally good combination is mixing a gold-stemmed bamboo (*Phyllostachys bambusoides* 'Holochrysa') with the Italian cypress (*Cupressus sempervirens*). These two plants create

The copper-leaved Plum introduces a nice extra colour into the garden (left); You have to be careful when choosing a conifer that it doesn't grow out of control. I like this *Thuja Smaragd* (right) as it behaves itself, it never needs to be pruned growing to about 3–4m (8–12') high with a 1m (3') spread.

Few things can give as much structure and movement to a garden as a bamboo (left); Good thing the *Cupressus sempervirens*, Italian Cypress, don't need to be pruned (right).

contrast with their differing textures and provide a completely evergreen screen. The bamboo is light and airy and moves gracefully even in the gentlest of breezes and the cypress remains majestic and stately in the sharpest of gusts.

Acacia dealbata (mimosa) is a striking, small evergreen tree, ideal as a feature plant in the right position in the garden. It requires full sun and shelter from the wind, so plant against a sheltered, south-facing wall. This Australian native produces masses of tiny pom-pom yellow flowers in late winter/early spring. There are many species and cultivars available but my favourite of all has to be *Acacia baileyana* 'Purpurea' for the stunning purple/blue colouring in its new leaves.

Evergreen plants are, of course, much loved by topiary gardeners – that is, gardeners who like to have fun making ornamental shapes out of their plants. Some of the more common plants used for this art form are *Buxus* (boxwood), *Lonicera* (honeysuckle) and *Taxus* (yew), but many evergreen plants can be used.

The beautiful feathery foliage of this purple/blue *Acacia* provides the perfect foil to the fluffy yellow flowers (right); You would need a big garden and a sense of fun! (below).

Not for you, you may think; however, the most common form of topiary is apparent in nearly all gardens in this part of the world. By pruning and shaping plants into a hedge, we are all practising this particular art form.

There are many different reasons to plant a hedge – to define the perimeter of the outdoor room or create little rooms inside the overall garden. Maybe you need a hedge for protection from the elements or from wandering animals or people. There is virtually no limit to what plants can be grown as a hedge, but when deciding on the right hedge for your situation, bear in mind these factors:

- height
- width
- exposure to wind
- evergreen or deciduous
- flowering or not
- native species
- maintenance.

The smallest of all hedges is probably the box hedge (*Buxus sempervirens*), which has traditionally been used to create definition between beds and other areas of a garden. For example, rose beds and herb gardens are often outlined by a box hedge. Many French chateaux and some of the great old gardens in England and Ireland would have had knot gardens, making up intricate patterns with box hedges and sometimes *Berberis* (barberry) hedges. If you want a slow-growing, dense, evergreen hedge that grows to about 50 cm, then *Buxus* is the one for you.

For coastal areas battered by salty gales, choosing a hedge can be a much more difficult job. Generally, plants that have a shiny, waxy leaf will be better suited to this situation because the waxy leaf affords protection by reducing water loss associated with the process of transpiration. Several plants to consider for a seaside location are: *Ilex* (holly), *Olearia* (daisy bush), *Crataegus* (hawthorn), and *Pinus* (pine). Pine is excellent for exposed areas because the tree produces needles that have a small surface area, so they lose less moisture than broad leaves. One very important thing to remember when choosing a hedge,

No plant can match *Buxus* (Box) if you want to create a low growing, dense, evergreen hedge, seen here at Bantry House in County Cork.

Christmas Rose

Black and White
is Not the Only Contrast

The importance of creating contrast in colour is an obvious and important principle in garden design, but equally important, and often overlooked, is contrast in texture and structure. To create an interesting garden, it is essential to sit contrasting plants beside one another. If you are stumbling or unsure about how to get the contrast of texture and colour right, then you can get help and inspiration from visiting other gardens.

3

the doctor says I need two or three more
months of treatment before the big one —
the high dose treatment that will precede
the transplant — and then, of course, the
transplant itself. I'm scared, but I know
that without this treatment there is a
high chance that I will not live . . .

To me these contrasting emotions sum up many parts of life. How many times do we want to achieve something but we are afraid of what we have to do to get there. Without fear we cannot understand safety. Without sadness we cannot understand happiness. Without pressure we cannot understand relief. At that moment, in January 1999, with the stem-cell transplant in sight, I was facing fear, sadness and pressure, with the goal of achieving safety, happiness and relief, oh such relief.

The natural world is also made up of many contrasts. Contrast in the garden isn't just a matter of colour contrasts. There are differences in texture and structure, light and darkness, damp patches and dry areas. The lime tree that I had come to love and hate as I gazed at it from my hospital window was full of contrasts – from the bare winter branches to the lushness of the green canopy in the summer.

It is true that however bad your own situation is, you don't have to look too far to see someone who is having it harder. No matter how tough this journey has been for me, no matter how hard I found it to overcome certain feelings and surmount the obstacles, things have worked out and will continue to work out, as I always knew, deep down, they would. I knew in my

heart I would be cured and I knew I was going to go on and live a full and healthy life. Perhaps most of my twenties were spent fighting a horrible illness but at least I had the opportunity to fight it and to beat it. I think that this has led to me being a better person. I am now – at the risk of it sounding like a cliché – very much more aware of how precious life is than I would have been if I hadn't had to go through this battle.

Figure 3
A, B, C
Photinia x fraseri 'Red Robin' with *Ilex altaclerensis* 'Golden King'
D, E, F
Taxus hedge
G *Clematis montana* growing in beech hedge
H Box hedge

Heucheras come in many varieties with fantastic names such as 'Crème Brulée', 'Tiramisu', 'Peach Flambé' and this one, 'Caramel'.

leaves, 'Quicksilver' produces an exotic red/orange stem of flowers about 2–2.5 m in length. Plant on its own in a gravel bed or plant it with *Heuchera villosa* 'Caramel'.

This *Heuchera* grows to about 30 cm, and produces lovely caramel-coloured, ruffled leaves. It also sends up soft plumes of baby's-breath-type flowers. This combination works because of the contrast in leaf types and also the subtle contrast in colour.

Even in a vegetable garden you can create attractive combinations. The

flower on the chive is a particularly attractive pink/purple ball of colour on top of thin, narrow stems. Why not plant this with some bronze fennel to give your veggie patch a blast of beauty?

A working kitchen garden can also be aesthetically pleasing, and even if you don't have space for a herb garden or vegetable plot, you can use this combination and other similar ones in an ornamental bed. As gardens are becoming smaller and smaller, it is important to remember that you don't

Bronze Fennel and Chives (above); Who says vegetable plants can't be ornamental (right).

have to have a dedicated plot for veggies or herbs, you can distribute your edible garden throughout your garden space to create contrasts of colour and texture.

Sun or Shade? That is the Question.

The natural world is full of contrasts and one of the most important is that between light and dark, sun and shade. This is nowhere more apparent than in the garden, where the question

Don't forget to mix these plants with others that will provide you with interest in seasons other than spring. Like *Euonymus fortunei* 'Emerald Gaeity', *Euonymus fortunei* 'Emerald 'n' Gold', with its lovely gold and green leaf, is a small evergreen shrub that provides foliage interest and colour throughout the year. And, again, don't forget the ornamental grasses, as they offer the garden so much in terms of leaf colour and movement and provide a constant contrast with the plants around them. For planting alongside the *Euonymous* shrubs, I would suggest smaller grasses like *Acorus gramineus* 'Ogon', *Carex hachijoensis* 'Evergold', *Uncinia rubra* and *Pennisetum alopecuroides* 'Little Bunny'.

Euonymus 'Emerald n Gold'.

You can just make out the red hue which develops over winter on the *Euonymus* 'Emerald Gaeity'.

What to plant is not the only consideration when designing a garden. All the different materials that we choose to employ affect the overall look and feel of the garden. With texture, colour and contrast in mind, let's look at these materials and decide which will work best in your garden design.

- Paving materials, such as natural stone or precast concrete, come in many different styles, sizes and colours. If you want a whimsical look in your garden, you might consider using precast concrete leaves or flowers to create a pathway, or if you prefer an 'at-one-with-nature' approach, go for the more natural stone.

Different paving materials – Timber decking can continue the theme of wooden floors inside the house into the garden.

You need to think about how a paved area is going to look in relation to the whole garden. Ask yourself, are all the different elements working together? Having a big seating area in all its splendour in the middle of a lawn can sometimes look like a UFO has just landed. The contrast between an area of grass and paving/decking/kerbing can be very stark. If you are intent on having paved space in the middle of your lawn, there are a few

things you can do to mellow the contrast. You can create an integrated look by placing plants between the hard area and the grass, which will provide a subtle transition. It will also make the hard landscaping look and feel more like part of the garden.

- Patios and decking come in a wide variety of styles and materials. Thinking of your garden as an outdoor room will help you decide on which material to use. Maybe you have timber floors inside the house, in which case it may work well to extend that look outside with timber decking. Alternatively, if you have a tiled floor indoors, continuing that style outside on the patio area may work well.

- Mulch is another material that we often use in gardens. Mulch is simply a term for any material that is spread on planted areas. Gardens need mulch for a number of reasons: to help retain water in the soil; to protect vulnerable roots from frost; to prevent weed growth. Some types of mulch even help to discourage certain pests, like slugs and snails. Cost alone should not determine the type of mulch we use in the garden, although, of course, it frequently is the deciding factor. Textures and contrasts should also be considered when we are choosing mulch.

- Ornamental gravel makes very attractive mulch and offers a wide variety of colours. Picture, for example, the dark foliage of *Ophiopogon*

planiscapus 'Nigrescens' growing in a bed mulched with some white or grey stone. This works very well because the stone has a harsh, heavy texture and a bright colour, while 'Nigrescens' offers a much softer appearance with its grass-like leaves and nearly black colour.

Gravels can look much tidier than the softer mulches, like bark, particularly in windy areas where the bark may fly around, leaving an untidy mess on paths and driveways. Gravels also tend to suit urban and suburban areas better than rural areas. However, if

Ophiopogon in white cobble.

you are using a lot of concrete materials and stone in the garden, then choosing ornamental gravel as mulch may create too harsh an effect. In that case, it may be better to go for a softer look by using another type of mulch.

- Bark, manure, compost and wood chippings can all be used as mulch and will create a softer, more natural-looking garden. They will also help to enrich the soil as they break down, adding humus and nutrients, and thus improving the soil's texture, structure and nutrient value. Bark mulch can look quite dark in a garden, so if you want to make your brightly coloured plants even more vibrant, give it a try. A group of spring-flowering daffodils can look even brighter in a bed of bark mulch, so, too, can white heathers. But if you don't like the look of bark mulch or gravel, or you want to choose another mulch for whatever reason, then a good quality compost (home-made or garden-centre bought) can give your garden a very smart, clean and natural appearance.

The dark bark mulch here acts as a perfect foil for the bright white heather.

Pieris japonica 'Debutante'

to Everything there is a Season

Each season offers a different kind of beauty from the very obvious yet transient flowers of summer to the elegant and subtle beauty of winter stems and twigs. Regal purple petals begin life as autumn bulbs, and scatterings of dancing wildflowers start as seeds in spring. Nature's original art gallery depends on the seasons, and the work of nature is a gardener's best friend.

4

For something a little different try *Callicarpa bodinieri var. giraldii* 'Profusion' (beauty berry). The clusters of deep pink berries produced by this plant look almost artificial (left).

of becoming endangered, so plant one if you have the space in your garden.

Early winter is the ideal time for designing new, and restructuring old, gardens and areas that may no longer give satisfaction. As the trees and shrubs begin to drop their leaves you can see the skeleton of the garden and the plants you need to work around. And anything that is planted now has the ideal opportunity to get established in the still warm, wet soil before actively coming into growth the following spring.

During the winter, it is time to lift and divide those perennial plants that may have outgrown their space, or perhaps are not flowering as well as they should be, due to overcrowding. Shrubs and trees that are in the wrong place and were screaming to be moved earlier in the year can all be replanted and replaced during this dormant season. A good idea for any gardener is to get into the habit of taking regular photographs of the garden. When you are planning what to do and what changes to make during the winter, it is very useful to have something to remind you of all those problems you encountered in the spring and summer months. Photographs taken throughout each season will do just that – jog the memory and remind you of that clump of perennial life lying beneath the soil or those shrubs that looked so wrong during the summer.

Dividing herbaceous plants like this *Hosta* is best done during the winter months when the plant is dormant (right).

Dividing plants

You can very easily bulk up on your plant numbers by dividing clumps of perennial plants that have died back for the winter. With a strong shovel or spade, lift the clump out of the ground, identify the growing shoots, and with a good sharp knife or spade, divide the plant so that each new division contains at least one shoot. These plants can then be grown on in pots or planted directly into the ground, where they will continue to prosper and multiply over the coming years. Or pass on some of these extra plants to friends and other interested gardeners. One of the great things about gardening is the passing on of knowledge, interest and surplus plants. I could not tell you how many plants I have in my garden that have been given to me as gifts, and every time I catch a glimpse of a certain plant it reminds me of the person who gave it to me. Sometimes the plant even outlives the benefactor, making the garden a truly living entity.

Using summer meadow flowers like these, in my sister, Deborah's garden creates a wonderful display and is of great benefit to conservation and wildlife.

beautiful long evenings. This time of year proves that good planning during the earlier seasons is the key. Summer-flowering shrubs, like the wonderfully scented lavender, should be planted around these seating areas, so that you can enjoy the heady fragrance as you soak up the afternoon sun rays.

There is another aspect of planting that needs to be remembered when thinking about summer in the garden. Simply put, will there be kids in your garden? Will your wonderful herbaceous specimens lose their heads, courtesy of a flying football? The garden is there

for the children to enjoy as much as the adults, but because we enjoy the outdoors in different ways, these spaces take a bit of planning. Maybe a play area could be incorporated into the design of your garden, or you might just want to leave a big area of lawn for a ball to be kicked about on. I am not saying that you cannot plant your trees and hedges in these areas, as most trees and hedges will take a certain amount of abuse, but consider which plants make the hardiest play-mates before sticking them in the ground. As your children grow older

you can start adding more tender shrubs and flowers to these areas.

They say our sense of smell is the sense most closely linked to memory and so it is no wonder that nothing conjures up a sense of summer like the smell of freshly cut grass. When it comes to grass, everyone has a preference. Maybe you want your grass area to be more meadow than putting green. If this is the case, then you will be actively encouraging more and more wildflower species to grow and you will only need to use the strimmer about twice in the year, leaving the grass cuttings where they fall so that the seeds can multiply.

Or maybe you are after the elusive, perfectly manicured lawn. If this is your dream, then you are in for a lot of maintenance during the summer. A good lawn tonic will have to be applied, and daisies, dandelions, clover, and other such undesirables, will need to be kept in check. The most environmentally friendly way of dealing with weeds is to remove them by hand. However, this is very rarely a feasible option because it is so time-consuming. The use of a selective weedkiller is the most effective and simple way of removing weeds – the word 'selective' referring to broadleaved weeds. These weedkillers will not kill grass or grass-type plants but they will kill any broadleaved plants that are growing in the lawn.

Moss is the other big scourge of lawns in this part of the world, and it is no wonder, as moss thrives in ground that is untilled, damp and warm. A number of things can be done to keep moss away, the main one being improving the surface drainage on a lawn. Many modern gardens have been compacted due to heavy machines working on the soil while the house was being built, and a few

Weeds on a lawn (top); Moss growing in a lawn (bottom).

69

less scrupulous builders will have left such hidden treasures as concrete blocks, leftover insulation materials, plastic containers and other such delights under the surface of the soil, none of which is conducive to creating ideal conditions for the perfect lawn. Digging over the soil and adding some organic matter such as compost and humus before laying the lawn will help a great deal.

Sulphate of iron mixed with water or used as lawn sand will help to keep moss away and there are many lawn food products available now that also contain a selective weedkiller and mosskiller. Applying this once or twice during late spring and summer will help keep the lawn in good condition.

Leaving aside annuals and summer bedding plants for the moment (they will be discussed in the next chapter), there is so much to choose from when it comes to other summer-flowering plants for the garden.

The aptly named butterfly bush (*Buddleia davidii*) is one of my favourites, producing large plumes of flowers in many different colours (depending on the variety), which are, as the common name suggests, very attractive to butterflies.

Hebes are worth their place in any garden because of their beautifully compact habit. They truly come into their own during the summer, producing masses of flowers ranging in colour from pure white through all the shades of pink to the deepest violet and blue.

Hydrangeas are another classic summer-flowering shrub. They come

Hydrangea arborescens 'Annabelle' produces large, airy, white flowers that brighten up even the darkest of areas.

Mock orange blossom (*Philadelphus*) is another plant that warrants a place in any garden that can accommodate it – it grows quite tall, up to 3 m with a similar spread. Strongly scented white flowers are produced during the summer on this deciduous shrub.

For late summer, few plants can beat *Caryopteris*, which produces beautiful, true blue flowers over grey-green leaves. The variety 'Worcester Gold' has golden yellow foliage. One of the most attractive things about this plant is its flowering period, coming into its best in late summer and autumn, when many other plants are coming to an end.

Fuchsia, grown in warmer parts as an outdoor plant and even as a hedge, is a particularly attractive shrub, producing masses of delicate flowers. It is only when you look closely at these

Philadelphus (above); The intense blue flowers of the *Caryopteris* make it an essential plant for the garden in September (right).

generally in several different varieties, and some are divided into two groups – mophead and lacecap. The former bears large mops of flowers, and the latter produces more delicate and open flower heads. One variety that is neither mophead nor lacecap is certainly one of my favourites.

There are so many varieties of *Fuchsia* to choose from. It is difficult to pick just one. They will all flower throughout the summer.

flowers that you really appreciate how exquisitely detailed they are. I wouldn't have a garden without at least one fuchsia. Look out for *Fuchsia* 'Sunray', with its stunning pink/purple foliage.

Other summer-flowering shrubs to look out for include:
Callistemon citrinus (crimson bottlebrush)
Cotinus coggygria 'Royal Purple' (smoke bush)
Abelia grandiflora 'Kaleidoscope'
Spiraea japonica 'Firelight'
Hypericum 'Hidcote' (St John's wort)

Herbaceous plants are at their very best during the summer months and are certainly among my favourite of all plants.

A Rose by Any Other Name

It is impossible to talk about summer-flowering shrubs without mentioning the king of them all, the rose. Roses have had very bad press over the years; people complain that they require a lot of care, but the truth is, they are not particularly high maintenance at all, they just need a little bit of TLC. A simple rule to follow: prune them hard in February and then again lightly as required during the summer and they will flower away freely for you. Check regularly for black spot, mildew and greenfly, all of which are easily treatable. Use liquid copper for most of the fungal problems (rust, mildew, black spot) and a good organic pesticide, or nematode, for the greenfly. With this relatively small amount of work, roses will give superb value to your garden year after year. Around 1,500 varieties of roses are available for purchase. They are divided into many groups and subgroups:

Hybrid Tea

Probably the most popular of all the groups, the hybrid tea rose will grow to 1–2 m high, with a spread of about 1 m. Each flower is produced individually at the end of each stem, as opposed to being produced in clusters. Many are scented, and they come in all colours and flower all summer long.

Floribundas

These roses produce flowers in clusters at the end of each stem, with each flower being smaller than the individual flowers of the hybrid tea rose. Growth habit and height and spread are all similar to the hybrid tea rose.

Patio Roses

Very small, patio roses grow only to about 40 cm in height and produce many clusters of flowers all summer long.

Standard Roses

The term 'standard' in this context simply means a plant that has been grafted on a clear stem. So it is with standard roses. Any rose can be grown as a standard, giving the effect of a clear stem to about 1.5 m, with the growth on top of the stem. This group is perfect for creating a bit of height in a bed.

David Austin Rose

Ground Cover Roses

As the name suggests, these roses will spread along the ground rather than grow tall. Most will have a spread of about 1 sq. m, not getting much higher than 40 cm. The flowers are normally quite small and simple. Many ground cover roses that are grown now are of the carpet rose type, which have been bred for ease of growing and are resistant to many of the pest and disease problems associated with roses.

Shrub Rose

Shrub roses are harder to define, being made up largely of roses that don't fall into any other group. They tend to be more vigorous and larger growing than the hybrid tea roses and floribundas, reaching up to 3 m in height. Good for hedgerows and poor soils.

Climber

Climbing roses will cover a good area of wall or fence if given the support of a trellis or wire. They prefer a south- or west-facing aspect and, like all roses, they need to be cut back before the end of February, to encourage them to flower all summer long.

Rambler

The stems of ramblers are not as rigid or self-supporting as those of climbing roses. Therefore, they are ideal plants to scramble up a tree or an old building. Ramblers produce masses of flowers on new stems that come from ground level each year. Their flowering period tends to be shorter than the other groups, with all their flowers being produced during a 4–6 week period.

David Austin Roses

David Austin is a specialist collector and grower of roses in England and he deserves a classification all to himself. Over 800 David Austin roses are available for purchase, all of them similar to the real old-fashioned English roses, grown for flower size, quality and scent.

Autumn

'Season of mists and mellow fruitfulness' – it is amazing how Keats's simple line manages to conjure up the spirit of autumn in the garden so magnificently. Autumn may be the time to begin putting the garden to bed, but it is also the time when the colours that do appear set the world on fire. Burnt orange buds and shiny red berries will create a backdrop worthy of any canvas.

You can have a fantastic display in the garden during the these months by using several types of plants – the late-flowering herbaceous plants; deciduous plants that show good autumn colour; evergreen plants with good leaf colour; plants laden with autumn berries; and grasses that offer great colour, movement and texture. A few good choices would be: *Echinacea, Hydrangea, Miscanthus, Pennisetum, Cosmos, Aster, Cotoneaster, Leucothoe, Heuchera* and *Eucomis*.

Miscanthus and *Pennisetum* are two grasses that really come into their own in the autumn months. They will have reached their full height by this time and before they go to bed for the winter their leaves change colour, producing amazing displays of copper, purple and orange-gold.

Heuchera and *Eucomis* are a fantastic plant combination for a small flowerbed or pot. They work very well together, showing off contrasting textures and complementing each other with their colouring.

I could not talk about autumn in the garden without mentioning the king of autumn colour – the Japanese maple. There are dozens of varieties of Japanese maple and you cannot go wrong with any of them as regards making a splash during the autumn months. Just make sure you have a spot sheltered from strong winds if you want to grow this treasure.

Hydrangeas, in particular, are terrific plants for autumn colour – but the colour depends on the soil. These plants are like the litmus paper of the plant world – their flowers turning blue in an acidic soil (low pH) and pink in limey soil (high pH).

One of the best plants for autumn colour is the Japanese Maple.

Contained Beauty

Containers should have a place in every garden; they can bring even the dullest of corners to colourful life. Don't think that just because your garden is a concrete slab or covered in timber decking or made of gravel that you cannot have a splash of colour. Working with pots and containers can often be one of the most pleasant ways to garden.

5

Pot with *Cordyline*, *Cyclamen* and *Hedera*.

later flowering *Primula*. A variety of spring bulbs (planted the previous autumn) will do well in late spring and these can eventually give way to the splendour of the summer bedding plants from about April/May onwards.

A mixture of different types of foliage plants, contrasting in colour and texture, can also work very well. A brilliant blue *Hosta* (plantain lily) with *Lysimachia nummularia* 'Goldilocks' (creeping Jenny) planted around the rim, for instance, will give your container interest during the summer months.

These are just a few suggestions of what to plant in your feature containers. There are as many combinations as there are plants in the world, so don't be scared to try something completely different and new. Use your own idea of colour combination to create an individual touch to your garden.

Practical Container

If your garden has a naturally high pH (limey soil) and thus will not grow ericaceous, or lime-hating, plants like camellias, rhododendrons, azaleas, some magnolias, and pieris, then containers are a godsend.

Containers allow you to control the environment completely, from soil type through to aspect. And since you are in control, it is important to get it right from the start.

reuse the pots and change the contents with the seasons. It is a good idea to feature a perennial in the centre of a large pot, such as *Cordyline australis* (cabbage palm), and work seasonal plants around the rim. For the seasonal interest, I would suggest *cyclamen* and *polyanthus* for the winter/early spring, changing to *Ranunculus* and then to

Ericaceous plants like this red *Camellia* will do better in a pot if your soil is limey.

Step 1: Use a good, ericaceous compost (high acidity), making sure that it has some loam (soil) content, so that it will not dry out too easily.

Step 2: Place your container in the correct position, ensuring that it is protected from wind, placing in sun or shade depending on which plants you are using, and making sure it is not going to become an obstacle, i.e. a trip hazard in the hours of darkness.

Step 3: Don't let the pot dry out!

Once you have followed these simple steps, you can stand back and admire the fruits of your labour. Step 3 is most important. Keep an eye on the moisture levels in your containers, because once a pot dries out, the plant has had it. All too often I hear people say that they thought their containers were getting enough water just by being left outside in the rain, but that is not the case. A container offers very restricted root room and a very limited reservoir of water, so it is vital that you make sure you are not relying

Scented lilies like this are a joy to all the senses during the summer (opposite).

solely on nature to provide your plants with a drink. Containers also offer a limited amount of nutrients and you need to keep an eye on the plants for any signs of hunger or deficiency, and treat it accordingly. If you are changing the plants from season to season, then it is easy to ensure they are getting nutrients by introducing fresh soil and compost each time you replant your pots. If, however, you are leaving a more permanent plant in the pot, you need to be rather more diligent. Deficiencies in iron and other nutrients will generally show up in the leaves – leaves turning yellow or curling or even falling off.

Camellias and *Rhododendrons* can suffer from a yellowing in the leaf, which is normally due to a lack of iron. Most other signs of stress in the leaf are caused by deficiencies of one form or another. Feeding the plants a few times a year with a good general plant food containing iron will help.

In July and August ericaceous plants produce the flower buds that will bloom the following spring, so it is during this July/August period that you need to feed them with potassium to promote setting buds. Sulphate of potash or tomato food or home-made compost with food ash works well. For most container plants, a regular feed with a good general purpose plant food throughout the year will be necessary. How regularly will be determined by which plant food you are using, so be sure to check the directions on the plant food container; feeding too much can do damage and not feeding often enough will be simply pointless. If this seems too much like hard work, then you can always incorporate a good slow-release plant food into the compost/soil in the pot. This will feed the soil for one full growing season.

Despite the extra care needed, there are few features in a garden that have as much impact as a pot full of bulbs in full flower, be it daffodils or tulips in spring or scented lilies in the summer.

When it comes to finding the right container for your garden, the choices are endless. Pots vary in colour, size, material and price – the last being especially true of handmade terracotta pots, the cost being all too frequently astronomical. But price should not be the only factor to be taken into consideration when you are choosing what to buy. Saving your hard-earned

Selection of different coloured pots.

money can sometimes be a false economy. Remember that you want these outdoor pots to last a lifetime, exposed to our climate, and that means you need good quality. When you think of the added beauty these containers will bring to your home, then the price begins to seem less important.

Pick a pot based on the colours of the plants you would like to put in it. Again, this is where personal taste comes in: you might want all the colours of the rainbow in your containers or you might want to keep with one very simple colour scheme.

Material too is important: terracotta, glazed ceramic, fibreclay, zinc and other metals, wood, terrazzo, plastic, and so on, are all used to make containers for the garden. Glazed pots come in a good variety of colours and offer protection against frosts and cold temperatures. Terracotta, on the other hand, is a porous material that absorbs water and expands when frozen, which can crack the pot. Some producers of terracotta pots today claim that they are now frost proof to a certain temperature, but I am not convinced. I am certainly not saying to avoid them entirely, but be aware of this problem if you are fan of the terracotta look.

On top of the vast range of pots that are commercially available, you can use your imagination. Literally

Clockwise from top left: Even an old tractor tyre can be put to use as a thing of beauty in the garden; Old chimney stacks are not much sought after as pots for the garden; Broken pots like these need not be thrown out. Leave them in place and fill with compost and a few bedding plants for a fabulous summer display.

anything that can store soil and water can work as a plant container. Old rubber tyres can make beautiful displays when planted.

Old sinks and troughs, baths, disused watering cans, Wellington boots, metal and plastic buckets also work well. I have even seen old teapots and

cups filled with bedding plants. Don't be in a huge rush to throw away broken pots either. I have a lovely pot standing proud amongst the shrubs and to look at it you would think it was perfect; however, on closer inspection you would see the gaping hole hidden at the back. In this way, a broken pot can be worked into planted areas where not all of the pot is visible, either lying on its side or with the broken part hidden from view. A pot or jug (broken or otherwise) lying on its side creates a wonderful look, with the flowers appearing to flow out of it. An old chimney-stack can also look fabulous settled into the middle of a garden.

- *Osteospermum* – another South African native, the cape daisy is one of the brightest and most cheerful of summer flowers, opening up in the daylight and closing each evening. Flowers are pink, purple, white, orange and yellow.
- *Bidens* – a lovely yellow flowering plant to complement the darker colours, use it to grow through the other plants in your container.
- *lobelia* (upright and trailing) – the traditional favourite for bedding schemes and containers. The upright form makes a great edging, and the trailing form produces masses of flowers all summer long in red, blue and white.
- *alyssum* – like the lobelia, alyssum has been grown for many years in bedding schemes and containers. Produces little hummocks of white or pink flowers.
- *antirrhinum* – one of the first plants I ever grew from seed and I still sow these seeds every March. I cannot imagine the summer without a potful of snapdragons! Technically a perennial plant, the snapdragon is grown as an annual, producing flowers that are a magnet for kids, who love to make the flower heads snap open and closed. Flowers are red, yellow, pink, white and orange.
- *gazania* – a sun-lover, the gazania has star-shaped, orange or yellow flowers that open in sunlight and close at night. Also a perennial plant that is often treated as an annual. Low growing and clump forming, the *gazania* will give colour right into the autumn.
- *nepeta* – *Nepeta hederacea*, referred to simply as trailing nepeta, is a variegated, white and green foliage plant. It has a quite distinctive minty fragrance, as it is a first cousin of *Nepeta faassenii*, or catmint. Acts as a great foil to the brighter and more colourful plants.
- *helichrysum* – grey, green and golden foliage, which can create some bulk in summer-planted containers. Acts as a good contrast to the more flowery plants.
- *Lysimachia* – also known as creeping Jenny, its golden foliage will trail down the side of a container. This plant will survive from year to year, creating a wonderful effect.

Most of the plants mentioned above are annual plants and will need to be replaced each year. Remove them around September/October and plant replacements for autumn/winter interest.

Bulbs

For the sake of simplicity, the word 'bulb' is used here as an umbrella term for all plants grown from bulbs, tubers, corms and rhizomes.

Talk of bulbs quickly conjures up pictures of spring-flowering plants like

Pot with *Pernettya*
and heather.

tulips and daffodils, yet there are
many summer-flowering bulbs – lilies,
begonias, gladioli, to name but a few.
Plant them from early March onwards
to provide flower colour from June
into September. When planting in a
pot or container, incorporate a bit of
grit under the bulb to ensure that it is
not sitting in water, which will cause
it to rot. Also remember to plant it at
a slight angle, so that the water will
not lodge in the bulb.

Autumn/Winter

For me, nothing quite sums up autumn
and winter in the garden like pots full
of cyclamen. From September/
October onwards, plant your cyclamen
to provide masses of colour during the
winter. Here again is where choosing
colour is important. Do you want a
red, green and white colour scheme for
Christmas, or something less specific?
Everyone seems to want these festive
colours in December but, come January,

A window box like this will provide masses of colour all summer long and can then be replanted to provide winter and spring colour (top); Bring colour to an otherwise blank fence or wall with pot holders or wall mounted baskets (bottom).

No Garden? No Problem.

Even if you don't have any garden at all, you can use containers to brighten up your space. So how do you make your patio or window ledge the talk of the neighbourhood all year round? With a small amount of work during the year, window boxes can provide twelve months of colour.

Pot-holders attached to an outside wall – very Mediterranean – can also add an extra dimension to an otherwise blank area; hanging baskets too.

Pots, baskets and window boxes can be attached to railings or balustrades enclosing paths, decks or patios. So, really, there is no outdoor area of your home that cannot provide colour when you start using pots and containers.

Digitalis species

Ancient Tradition: Modern Remedy

We tend to think of the healing powers of herbs and herbal remedies as old wives' tales: harmless, cute, but ultimately ineffective. However, most modern medical drugs can be traced back to these ancient remedies. Herbal remedies have been used in Ireland since at least medieval times and much earlier in other parts of the world.

6

The side-effects of the drugs are harsh
and make me nauseous; it is tough going.
Every week now I visit a reflexologist to help
my body deal with the drugs. This treatment
is very helpful and I find his knowledge of
alternative treatments fascinating. I wonder
more and more about the benefits of 'alternative'
medicine, as opposed to 'conventional' medicine.
An alternative way of healing the whole person,
with the use of herbal remedies and treatments
like acupuncture and reflexology. This approach
is certainly worth a try.

We tend to think of the healing powers of herbs and herbal remedies as old wives' tales: harmless, cute, but ultimately ineffective. However, most modern medical drugs can be traced back to these ancient remedies.

My interest in 'alternative' medicine developed when I was ill and undergoing conventional treatment. I began to attend reflexology treatment and acupuncture to help me cope. I use quotation marks around the word *alternative* because I don't like the use of the term in this context. I believe, in fact, that modern medicine is the 'alternative'.

Some treatments date back thousands of years – herbal remedies have been used in Ireland since at least medieval times and much earlier in other parts of the world. Traditional Chinese medicine, widely accepted and practised in the Far East, is grounded in a holistic orientation to health and life and influenced by the belief that human beings are intimately connected to the environment and the universe, and that a harmonious relationship should exist between them. Such medicine cannot prevent every illness from occurring, of course, but its philosophical approach to health and life makes a great deal of sense to me.

Herb Garden

Herb lovers will delight in the variety of herbs available on the market.

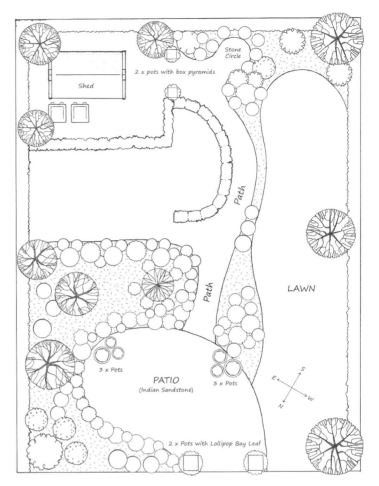

Figure 6

Indeed, so many are available in Ireland today that the subject would require a book of its own. However, I do want to mention a few general tips to make sure that the herbs you decide to grow thrive. Most herbs that we grow in this part of the world are native to the Mediterranean region. Bear this in mind when you plant them. If you are planning a herb bed in your garden, or if you want to grow herbs in pots, remember

Put bird feeders in the garden and sit back to enjoy the show.

(a washing-up bowl set into the ground will do), which will enable frogs to spawn. They will return the favour by eating slugs and snails.

- When natural food sources are scarce, you can give the birds a helping hand by putting out a variety of nuts, seeds and fat snacks. Don't worry about them filling up too much on the tasty snacks you provide, they are guaranteed to want the bugs and aphids on apple trees for dessert.

Keeping your garden healthy and organic all year round is beneficial for the plants you grow and the insects that protect them. Reduce the use of chemicals, particularly to control insects. So instead of spraying first and asking questions later, why not try hand picking and removing weak plants that are heavily infested with pests, and also employing some of nature's own pest killers, like ladybirds, to try to solve the problem without chemicals.

Interesting Uses for Herbs and Other Plants

Whether or not you are growing plants for their culinary use or for their medicinal properties, the botanical world harbours some species that are simultaneously saviours and villains. The foxglove (*Digitalis*), for example, is a common hedgerow plant that is used in the preparation of digoxin.

A white and a purple foxglove *Digitalis*. The extract from this plant is used by millions worldwide every day in the drug Digoxion (left); All parts of the Yew tree are used in the manufacture of the chemotherapy drug Taxol (right).

Millions of people are treated every day with this drug for various heart conditions. In the correct dosages, this attractive plant can save lives, but high doses can be lethal.

The Irish yew (*Taxus baccata* 'Fastigiata') is another plant that has had a profoundly beneficial impact on medicine in the last decade. Although this attractive shrub produces bright red berries with poisonous seeds, the extract from the *Taxus* is used effectively in the chemotherapy drug Taxol.

Echinacea purpurea may be more familiar to people these days in tablet form, taken to boost their immune system and keep colds and flu away. Yet in its natural form it is a most striking herbaceous plant with very dramatic pink or white flowers, which positively ignore the rain and stand proud in the autumn before they go for

Wormeries

Wormeries, or worm bins, are a great way to work with nature to ensure your soil is perfect. Worms are the unsung heroes of our garden: they do your composting by eating the peelings and scraps, as well as the bacteria and moulds that have formed on the waste material.

Once they've finished feasting, the worms produce worm casts, which are perfect for enriching the soil.

It is quite simple to make a home-made box that can be filled with a bedding of organic matter, such as damp brown leaves, sawdust, clean wood shavings, or shredded paper. Or you can buy one of the many ready-made wormeries available on the market. The worms themselves – tiger worms – can also be bought by the kilo, and will turn your kitchen waste, and the bedding material you have provided them with, into high quality compost suitable for use in your garden or for your house plants.

When putting scraps into the worm bin, be sure to bury the food waste in the bedding, to prevent flies and odours. After nine to twelve months, the compost will be partially finished and it is time to move it to one side of the bin, where it can be left to age. Add new bedding to the empty half of the bin, and begin the process again. In approximately six weeks the worms will move to the new bedding and leave the aged compost ready for use in the garden.

Most purpose-built wormeries are designed on the three-tray model, starting with the base tray, where the worms begin feasting on your kitchen waste. When this tray is full, you simply place the next tray on top of it, and when the worms have finished regurgitating the waste in the base tray, they will make their way up into it. When the second tray is full, you place the third tray on top. The principle being that by the time the third tray is full, the compost in base tray should be ready to use on your garden, at which point you can begin the rotation over again. The compost, or worm casts, produced is one of the richest and most beneficial composts of all.

The worms will eat nearly all types of kitchen waste, but keep an close eye on the pH

level – the worms like the level to be close to neutral (7). (A pH meter will give you a reading.) If the waste is too acidic, you will not see much worm activity when you lift the lid. For example, onions, garlic and peppers are all quite acidic and should only be added in moderation. I have also discovered that worms are not that partial to leftover prawn Szechuan! So just stick with blander foods, until you get a good idea of what your worms prefer. Also avoid using citrus peels and any perennial weed roots.

Green Cone

Another good option for the small or large garden is the green cone. This aptly named composter is one of the simplest systems for food waste disposal available on the market. The sealed, cone-shaped device is buried halfway into the ground. Just add the food waste and close the lid. Composting in these green cones does not require any work on your part – no turning or shovelling – all that is required is to leave the compost for six months, and then you can start taking the finished compost from the bottom of the pile. Or after the six-month period, empty the compost into a trench, cover with soil and boards to prevent animals from getting at it, and leave it for about a month, by which time the freshest compost will have sufficiently decomposed to allow you to use it in the garden. On the other hand, you could always have two green cones on the go at once, and operate them along the lines of the twin compost bin (see above).

Bokashi

Not only is 'bokashi' a fun word to say, it is also a useful, relatively bad-odour free means of disposing of your household scraps. Perfect for the no-garden gardener, the bokashi method ferments your food waste, as opposed to decomposing it, with the result that the smell produced is less offensive than composting, and the waste bucket can be kept in the kitchen for easy access.

The Japanese term 'bokashi' is usually associated with fermented wheat or rice bran, which is created very simply by using effective microbes, known as EM. Bokashi can be made – the recipe contains wheat bran, molasses, EM and water – or purchased on its own, or with a bokashi kit, complete with instructions on successful bokashi composting and bucket with a tap to drain off excess liquid.

Bokashi composting requires you to use alternate layers of kitchen scraps (including cooked meats and fish) and the bokashi mixture until the bucket is filled. The mixture is then left to ferment for up to ten days, when it can be dug into your garden or into your compost pile to decompose further. Like other composting arrangements mentioned previously, it is a good idea to have two bokashi buckets on the go, so that when one bucket is full and the ten-day fermentation is taking place, you can be filling the second one.

The fermented matter that is produced by bokashi composting is rich in nutrients that will benefit any plants in your garden or in your window box that require nutrient-rich soil.

NB: If you decide to make your own bokashi composter, then use a large plastic bucket with a tap, or line the bottom of a bucket with a layer of absorbent material such as newspaper, sawdust or peat, to soak up the liquid.

the Edible Garden

Home-grown fruit and veg, or produce straight from a good farmers' market, tastes so much better than the mass-produced kind. And I strongly suspect that it is also the healthier option.
You really should try to grow some yourself. You will be amazed at the returns you will get from a small financial outlay, a bit of enthusiasm and some good manure!

7

plants outside for a few hours every day, extending the period slightly each day. Don't be put off by any of the technical terms, it is all really quite simple.

Once your seedlings are hardened off, it is time to transplant them in the prepared vegetable patch.

Going Organic

When you are growing your own fruit and vegetables, you are the one who is in control. It is a great opportunity to go organic, so make sure you only use organic products.

For the soil preparation, use well-rotted manure or an organic compost and leaf mould (see above).

If you need something to control pests and diseases later in the year, then use organic pesticides and fungicides, or try a biological pest control. Biological controls are insects, some microscopic, that are introduced to control pests attacking crops. For example, tiny little nematodes, such as *Phasmarhabditis hermaphrodita*, will devour any slugs and snails in the garden, and the parasitic wasp *Encarsia formosa* will control many types of whitefly. They feed voraciously on whitefly and will die off themselves when the whitefly are gone. If you have not tried this approach before, then maybe this is the year to give it a go.

You can also control several pests

Even brambles like this can be a feast for thousands of greenfly.

by careful planting; marigolds, for example, will keep aphids away, so plant these throughout your vegetable plot. Protective 'companions' for your roses, garlic and chives keep the aphids away from the garden's natural perfume provider.

It is important to try to be as organic as possible, especially in the edible garden. But I am realistic about this. I use things like horse and farmyard manure even if I cannot prove that the livestock which produced it were reared 100 per cent organically. To achieve an utterly organic approach (while not to be discouraged) is a near impossibility for the amateur gardener

Marigolds like this are a great companion plant to deter aphids.

and certainly takes the fun out of kitchen gardening.

Fruit and Nut Trees

Fruit trees can be beautiful as well as healthy additions to your garden and can integrate well amongst flowers and vegetables alike. Our damp northern weather is not suited to all types of fruit trees, but cherry, pear, and apple can do well in the Irish climate.

Cherry

If you are looking to plant a cherry tree, for eating try *Prunus avium* 'Stella' and for cooking *Prunus cerasus* 'Morello'. 'Stella' is a sweet cherry variety with large dark, juicy fruit that is ready for eating in late July. A sweet variety that produces fruit early in the season is *Prunus avium* 'Early Rivers'. 'Morello' produces sour cherries, which are ideal for cooking or making cherry brandy. These

Cherries ripening on the tree.

attractive and delicious fruit providers like to be grown by a south-facing wall – the heat trapped by the wall helping the fruit to ripen.

Pear

If you are a lover of the luscious pear, then give the 'Conference' pear (*Pyrus cummunis*) a try. It is self-fertile but, as with many self-fertile varieties of fruit, it tends to crop better if planted with another variety. As a companion for the 'Conference', plant *Pyrus cummunis* 'Doyenné du Comice', which in turn will produce a delicious dessert pear.

Pears growing on a tree like this in Ireland will probably have to be brought in during late September to ripen inside.

Apple

Apple trees look attractive all year round, with their pretty spring blossoms giving way to juicy apples in autumn; even their bare branches create a lovely winter scene. They are a great addition to any garden that has a bit of space and sunlight and are adaptable to most soil conditions.

When choosing an apple tree to plant, you must first decide whether you want cooking or eating (dessert) apples. Hundreds of different apple trees will grow well in the Irish climate and the choice will come down to your eating preference. If you prefer your dessert apples sweet and juicy, then try the famed 'Cox's Orange Pippin' (*Malus domestica*), which can be eaten from September to January, or its close relative 'Fiesta', which is just as tasty and keeps a bit longer (producing fruit right up to November), or maybe the honey-flavoured 'Jonagold'.

If you prefer an eating apple with more tartness and acidity, choose the early fruiting and disease resistant 'Discovery', which can be eaten from late August, or the luscious yellow 'Greensleeves' variety, which is harvested in October.

All these apple varieties require a pollination partner to be planted at the same time in order for them to produce fruit. The pollination partner must be a different variety of the same

fruit species, which flowers at about the same time. Varieties are broken down into three groups, depending on their flowering period – early, medium, and late. For successful pollination, you will need to plant two or more from the same group (triploid varieties need two pollinators for best results).

Apples are packed full of goodness and are relatively easy to grow. When you are used to eating apples fresh from the tree you will never be satisfied with a shop-bought apple again.

Early Season Flowering

Egremont Russet

Lord Lambourne

Rev. W. Wilks

Ribston Pippin (triploid)

St. Edmund's Russet

Mid Season Flowering

Beauty of Bath

Blenheim Orange (triploid)

Bramley's Seedling (triploid)

Charles Ross

Cox's Orange Pippin

Crispin (triploid)

Discovery

Gala/Royal Gala

Golden Russet

Greensleeves

Grenadier

Granny Smith

Holstein (triploid)

James Grieve

Jonagold/Jonagored

Katy

Worcester Pearmain

Late Season Flowering

Falstaff and Red Falstaff

Golden Delicious

Red Devil

Laxton's Superb

Elstar

Golden Delicious

For culinary or cooking apples, the best bet is 'Bramley's Seedling', and as it is a triploid, it needs two pollinators for best results. Try 'Howgate Wonder' or 'Bountiful', or you could also try a variety of crab apple, which are good pollinators for all the other apple varieties. They have a beautiful apple blossom in the spring, fantastic autumn colour, and tasty fruits in winter. They are a real treat in the garden, as they have three seasons of interest: they pollinate eating and cooking apples; provide you with the ingredient for delicious crab apple jelly; and also provide the birds with a bountiful food source in the winter months. Try planting, *Malus* 'John Downie', *Malus robusta* 'Red Sentinel', or one of my favourites, *Malus* 'Royalty'.

The ideal time to plant your apple trees is during the winter months – November to February is best. Like cherry trees, it is preferable to plant apple trees in a south-facing section of the garden that gets a lot of sun; however, a west-facing location will also work. Apple trees need to be sheltered but not suffocated – ideally, the tree should be planted in a spot that is protected from blustery winds, which can harm the fruit and keep away the pollinating insects, but still have enough air circulation around it to prevent it from developing moulds. It is equally important to ensure that

The pollination of apple trees is carried out by insects, especially bees. Bearing this in mind, it is a good idea to plant species near the trees that will attract bees and thus help pollination. In many of the monastic fruit gardens, lemon balm was planted for this purpose, as this plant is terrific for attracting bees and other pollinating insects. The garden centre supplying you with your trees will also be able to supply you with suitable pollination partners, or with a self-fertile variety.

There are few things nicer in the kitchen garden than eating peas fresh from the plant (right); All brassicas like these Brussels sprouts need plenty of nutrient and well drained soil (below).

and early summer peas, like beans, prefer full sun and well-drained soil. There are numerous varieties of pea: mangetout, sugarsnap, garden pea and petit pois.

These delicious additions to your edible garden should be planted from seed in early spring (set about 2.5–10 cm apart) and you will have fresh peas in approximately 10–12 weeks. Read each seed packet for specific planting instructions.

Brassicas

Broccoli, Brussels sprouts, cabbage and cauliflower are some of the best-known brassicas. Ready for harvest in the cool months of the year, brassicas are the powerhouse of the vegetable world because of the antioxidants contained in each flavour-filled bite. If you planted peas or beans earlier in the season, then you can replace these plants with brassicas to keep your crops healthy and your garden in 'bloom' all year round.

Broccoli, Brussels sprouts and

Freshly harvested turnip.

cabbage can be seeded from the early summer until well into autumn, just be sure they are seeded at least four to six weeks before the first frost. If you are opting to plant them from seedlings, then be sure to harden them off outdoors in a sheltered spot for a week before putting them in the ground. Brassicas are best suited to a limey soil that is rich in nutrients and well drained.

Root Vegetables

The mother of all Irish root vegetables is the potato, but there are many other root vegetables that grow well in our soil. Radishes, beetroot and carrots, turnips and parsnips are all earth dwellers that do well in Irish soil.

Root vegetables are cold weather veggies that may be planted in early spring and left in the garden until autumn. They prefer a loose soil that allows their roots room to spread and, apart from beetroot which can be slow to germinate, they are best grown from seed. Radishes and turnips can be planted in the spring and again in late summer for two good crops. Radishes will be ready to eat after three or four weeks, but turnips take longer to reach a good size for eating.

Turnips, as well as beets, should be harvested as soon as they are a good size – don't let them become overgrown. Parsnips, however, can remain in the ground until late autumn without their taste being impaired.

In ancient times it was believed that potatoes were the food of the devil, as they grew underground and downwards towards hell. Thankfully that belief has died out – I cannot imagine life without the spud.

General Tips for Veggie Success

1. Plan the vegetable patch well. Draw up a rough design showing what you want to grow and where you want to grow it, and make a rough calendar of when to do each job.

2. Do all the preparatory work over the winter. Incorporate good quality organic matter and well-rotted manure, dig into the soil and let the frost break it down.

3. Where possible, use disease resistant varieties of plants, thus reducing the need for any types of control and, if necessary, use biological controls to eradicate pests and disease.

4. Attract pollinators into the garden by planting attractive flowering plants. Attract birds into the garden with feeders and berried plants; they will keep slugs and snails in check.

5. Use a wormery to compost your kitchen and vegetable waste. This will compost your waste relatively quickly and provide you with a valuable supply of worm casts, which are incredibly good for aiding plant growth.

6. Stagger planting and sowing. When you are sowing vegetable seeds, sow a certain amount day one, leave for about two weeks and then sow some more, and so on. The vegetables will mature over a longer period, extending the harvest time and thus giving you a much longer supply of fresh veg.

Edible City

While city living may be convenient, there is often little space for a kitchen garden, certainly a large one. However, growing your own fresh vegetables is still an option; it can be done on a smaller scale. If you fancy a home-grown salad, you can grow your own gourmet greens (and reds) in your back patio or on your window sill. A long window box will allow you to grow lettuce leaves, spinach, radishes, chives, and even tumbler tomatoes. Just give your plants enough space in the container to avoid the spread of diseases. With daily attention you can keep the plants pest free – spray with water to get rid of aphids and pick off any other pests by hand.

Young vegetable plants can be purchased from your local garden centre in April/May, or you can try growing them from seed indoors from as early as February. Find a sunny location for your salad box, keep it well watered and watch it grow. Harvest when the plants are ready, and cut back the lettuce and spinach to keep them growing well into the summer.

Tools for Pruning

It is important when choosing pruning tools, such as a hedge shears, to purchase either carbon steel or stainless steel tools made by a good manufacturer. Lesser metals will corrode and chip and are not as easy to clean and maintain. Cheaper models will also loosen at the cutting joint leading to a messy cut, which can damage the plants. Try the tools out for weight and size before you purchase them to make sure that you are comfortable with them. Bear all this in mind when choosing any pruning tool such as:

- hedge shears
- lopper
- extension lopper
- box pruner

Finally, I would urge you once again to invest in the better quality tools, as a good tool is something you should need to buy only once (unless, like me, you keep losing them!), whereas a cheap tool will cost you more in the long run, as you will need to keep replacing it.

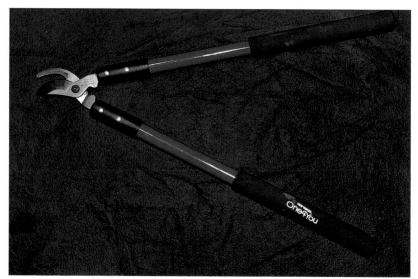

My Favourite Plants

Chapter 1

Himalayan birch
(*Betula utilis* var. *jacquemontii*)
This is probably my favourite of all trees because of everything it offers. Its stunning white bark, which improves with age, and its slender and graceful form are two of the main features of its beauty. However, it offers much more than that: fantastic, vivid yellow autumn colour, followed in the depths of winter by attractive catkins, which hang from the branches. This tree will grow to about 6 m high and a spread of 2–3 m. It can be grown as a single stem specimen, which produces striking silver bark, or as a multi-stem, with more than one stem growing from ground level to create an informal effect.

Midland hawthorn
(*Crataegus laevigata* 'Paul's Scarlet')
If gardening is about encouraging wildlife into the garden, then look no further than this hawthorn when choosing a tree. The lovely red flowers of this variety attract bees and other insects; the berries provide food for the birds in the winter; and the thorny branches offer refuge for birds to build their nests. At a height of approximately 5 m and a spread of around 2 m, this tree is a suitable for a modest-sized garden.

Mountain ash/Rowan
(*Sorbus aucuparia*)
The mountain ash is an ideal tree for a small garden, only reaching 5–6 m in height with a spread of about 2–3 m. But it also warrants a place in the garden for many other reasons. It has more than one season of interest, providing flowers during summer, beautiful red autumn foliage later in the year, followed by masses of brightly coloured berries – red, orange, pink, yellow or white, depending on the variety. These berries are a very welcome form of sustenance to many birds during the winter months.

Whitebeam (*Sorbus aria* 'Lutescens')
One of the real delights of spring in the garden is watching whitebeam buds blast into leaf. The colour literally changes by the hour as the leaves unfurl and meet the spring light. As a mature tree, it can reach about 5 m, with a spread of about 3 m. It keeps a compact, rounded shape, making it an ideal choice for a smaller or medium-sized garden. It flowers during late spring, although you have to look closely to see the blooms against the silver-green foliage. The orange-red berries in the autumn and winter provide nourishment for many bird species.

Himalayan Birch

Mountain Ash/Rowan

Chapter 2

Cherry plum tree
(*Prunus cerasifera* 'Nigra')
This medium-sized tree is a great addition to any garden, with its beautiful purple/copper foliage, which is produced in spring after the tree has covered itself in numerous, small, baby pink (nearly white) blossoms. Some trees will produce small ornamental, plum-like fruit, which is valuable to birds. Very easy to trim back and keep as a hedge. If left unpruned, it can grow to 8–10 m in height.

Daisy bush (*Olearia*)
The daisy bush is an evergreen shrub with holly-like, dark green leaves, which provide a mellow green hue to the garden all year round. Best grown in mild conditions, the daisy bush produces masses of white, daisy-like flowers in July that almost obscure its prickly leaves. Growing to a maximum height of around 4 m, an adult daisy bush will act as a superb windbreak in any seaside garden, with its dense foliage and love of mild, salty air.

Escallonia
For a versatile shrub that is excellent for use as a seaside border or hedge, the *Escallonia*, with its attractive glossy green leaves, is a lovely choice. There are many varieties of *Escallonia*, which produce blossoms in colours ranging from pink and white to crimson throughout the summer months. It matures into a very attractive shrub or hedge, with its flowers attracting butterflies during the summer. There are also a few yellow-leaved varieties such as *Escallonia laevis* 'Gold Brian'. Growing to 2–3m in height, these shrubs can be pruned to a tidy height of 1 m and under.

Firethorn (*Pyracantha*)
This fiery-coloured plant is ideal for planting as hedges or along walls for a gorgeous display of summer flowers and later, winter berries. These vigorous evergreens do well in most soil types in part shade to full sun. They will grow to 1.8–3 m and are especially useful as a security barrier if planted as a hedge, as the thorns they produce are more effective than any barbed wire.

Golden Bamboo
One of the most striking in the bamboo family, *Phyllostachys bambusoides* 'Holochrysa', or 'Allgold', is a large, clump-forming plant that will grow to over 6 m in height. The stunning golden canes are thicker than most bamboo canes (up to 4 cm in circumference), starting out a buttery yellow and eventually maturing to bright gold. Best grown in a well-drained soil, this exotic-looking feature plant

Escallonia

Golden Bamboo

prefers warm climates (Ireland's climate is warm enough) and partial shade.

Holly (*Ilex*)

Holly is one of the most versatile feature plants of the evergreen garden. It can be clipped into hedges, grown as tall shrubs, or shaped to form archways or topiaries. There are dozens of varieties on the market but be sure when you are planting that you plant a male and a female plant, as both are needed to produce the winter berries that the shrub is famed for. Some self-fertile varieties are available, such as *Ilex aquifolium* 'J.C. van Tol' and *Ilex aquifolium* 'Pyramidalis', which will produce berries even if they are planted individually. Some varieties have the common prickly, waxy-looking green leaves and others have smooth-edged, variegated leaves. Holly plants grow large but can be pruned aggressively to a desired size. Be sure to place your holly where it will receive maximum sunlight.

Italian cypress

(*Cupressus sempervirens*)

This elegant, column-like tree is ideal for evoking a summer in the Mediterranean. Suitable for most soil types, the Italian cypress will provide a classic line to the backdrop of any garden. Make sure you have enough space for this lovely, dark green-leafed tree, as it will grow quite tall (20 m), although only spread under 1 m in width approximately. Makes an ideal screen for sound or wind. Because of its very narrow habit and a root system that is not too vigorous, this tree is ideal for planting right next to a building or a wall. Grow in full sun and well-prepared soil for best results. Italian cypress should not be pruned, as it can be susceptible to pests.

Mimosa (*Acacia dealbata*)

Stunning yellow spring flowers and ferny green foliage make this compact tree the perfect accent plant for any garden. Year-round evergreen foliage makes it an ideal architectural plant to provide colour and screening. Growing to between 3–8 m in height, the mimosa is suitable for container growing or for positioning in full sun and drought-prone soils. This tender evergreen can be pruned back yearly to restrict size. It will need protection from strong winds and severe frosts.

Photinia fraseri 'Red Robin'

This dense evergreen shrub grows equally well as a specimen shrub or as a hedge. The new growth on the plant is a lovely red colour, which contrasts beautifully with the dark green older leaves. The foliage stays looking attractive for twelve months of the year, but cut it back in early March to keep it dense and bushy and to get the

Holly

Photinia (Red Robin)

best red colour. If left unchecked, it can reach a height of 3–4 m and a spread of 2–3 m, but it makes a much more attractive plant if kept pruned.

Pine

The genus *Pinus* encompasses over 100 different species, all of which are evergreen trees with needle-like leaves. They vary in height, from under 1 m (*Pinus mugo* – dwarf mountain pine) to 25 m and more (*Pinus sylvestris* – Scots pine). They nearly all produce cones (tory tops), containing seeds that are much-loved by squirrels and other wildlife. The resin of several varieties is used to produce turpentine. *Pinus* is a valuable tree in this part of the world for many reasons, one being its suitability to coastal gardens.

White cedar

(*Thuja occidentalis* 'Smaragd')
An attractive conifer growing to about 4–5 m with a spread of 1–1.5 m, the white cedar is a compact conical tree with upright sprays of mid-green leaves. Forming a nice shape as it matures, it is a hardy plant that will do well in most soil types, even chalky lime, provided they are moist and well-drained and the tree is planted in a full sun position. What I like about this plant is that it keeps a good compact shape and it does not grow out of hand, with no need for pruning, and apart from watering in its first

year, it requires pretty much zero maintenance.

Chapter 3

Beschorneria yuccoides 'Quicksilver'

This yucca-like plant is an exotic garden showpiece with fleshy, grey-green leaves which, once the plant is established, will produce great bursts of gorgeous red, pink and orange flowers in the summer months. These outrageous blooms appear at the ends of red stems, which can grow to over 2 m. Likes a sunny, well-drained position and can withstand temperatures down to zero degrees Celsius.

Hebe (veronica)

A stunning genus, *Hebe* is perfect for an area of your garden that is part shade to full sun. This evergreen shrub produces plentiful spikes of flowers in early to mid-summer, ranging in colour from white through pink to the deepest violet and even blue. Because of its size (up to 60 cm high and wide), *hebe* makes an attractive border or show plant. It can be planted from seed and likes to be fertilized in spring before new growth begins. Prune after flowering. *Hebe* is one of several shrubs that can get 'leggy' if not cut back each year.

Heuchera villosa 'Caramel'

Heuchera is a popular groundcover

Pine

Hebe

plant that comes in a wealth of foliage colours, with blooms that make a powerful impact on any garden. *Heuchera villosa* 'Caramel' is a particularly lovely variety, with its silky, caramel-coloured foliage, which grows equally well in sun or part shade. Varieties of *Heuchera* thrive in moist, well-drained, organic-enriched soils. A hardy plant, 'Caramel' is an ideal perennial for the garden beginner. It flowers from April to June.

Japanese rush
(*Acorus gramineus* 'Ogon')
The boggy-soil-loving Japanese rush is grown especially for its golden foliage. Evergreen, this hardy grass will withstand all but the harshest of winters. Suitable for planting in damp conditions, including water features and containers, the Japanese rush should be divided from March to May.

Chapter 4

Abelia grandiflora 'Kaleidoscope'
This hardy, slow-growing, medium-sized shrub produces perfect white, lightly scented flowers from June to October. It is a relatively compact shrub that is ideal for any small to medium-sized garden. Suited to mild temperatures, *Abelia* is happiest in sunny conditions and well-drained soil. The variegated leaves change colour with the seasons, from a vibrant yellow and green to a darker green in summer and then bursting with colour in the autumn with red stems and abundant white flowers.

Angel's fishing rod (*Dierama*)
Angel's fishing rod is one of the stars of the summer garden. Growing to about 2–3 m in height, this plant produces long arching stems with thimble-like flowers, which give the effect of a fishing rod bending into the water. Native to South Africa, the *Dierama* will grow in most soil types, providing it receives enough sunlight. Position it behind a plant that is more ornamental all year round, as when not in flower the *Dierama* looks like an untidy clump of grass.

Aster
The aster is among the loveliest of flowering perennials for the beginner gardener. All varieties provide excellent late colour to any herbaceous border or other area of the garden. They grow well in most soil types and thrive in full sun. Some of the taller varieties will need staking, but the more compact varieties, such as the long-flowering *Aster frikartii*, will grow tall and straight naturally. Although very susceptible to developing mildew on their stems in our warm, damp conditions, several species are mildew resistant, such as *Aster frikartii* 'Mönch' (Michaelmas daisy).

Beauty berry
(*Callicarpa bodinieri* var. *giraldini* 'Profusion')

The beauty berry is aptly named, producing a 'profusion' of glossy, bead-like, purple berries in mid-autumn. Shortly after the berries appear, the leaves will drop, leaving a stunning contrast of stark branch and rich, almost artificial-looking, coloured berries. The berries are classed as inedible and many animals don't like them; however, nobody told the birds that. This plant will remain a showpiece in the winter garden until the temperatures drop and then the hungry birds will descend and strip the branches bare. It does well in most soils but prefers a humus-rich, acidic, well-drained soil.

Butterfly bush
(*Buddleia davidii*)

This beautiful, deciduous shrub appeals to more than just butterflies, although they do flock to this plant on warm summer days. From July to August it produces attractive flowers, ranging in colour from pure white through different shades of pink to the deepest purple. It grows best in a sunny, well-drained position to a height of 3 m, with a 3 m spread, and needs to be cut back before the start of March. It also grows well in containers and can be used for elegant cut flowers.

Cosmos

There are many varieties and colours of this popular, late-summer flowering, including the lovely white *Cosmos bipinnatus* 'Purity' and the uniquely shaped *Cosmos bipinnatus* 'Sea Shells'. A hardy plant that flourishes in full sunlight, *cosmos* prefers a light soil that is moist and well drained. Be sure to stake plants early in the season and then deadhead regularly to keep them in bloom. Excellent for cut flowers from June through to October. For a dramatic effect, try the perennial chocolate-scented *Cosmos atrosanguineus*. This wonderful plant, which is ideally grown in a pot, produces masses of dark brown, almost black flowers that actually smell of dark chocolate on hot sunny days.

Cotoneaster

Species of the genus *Cotoneaster* vary hugely in height, spread and habit. The lowest growing forms like *Cotoneaster congestus* or *Cotoneaster procumbens* 'Queen of Carpets' reach no height at all but hug the ground, forming a mat of stems and green leaves. At the other end of the scale, *Cotoneaster* 'Cornubia' can grow into a medium-sized tree of about 6–8 m in height. All *cotoneasters* have in common beautiful white flowers in spring and summer, good autumn colour, which is very unusual in an evergreen plant, and then lovely berries, normally red, in winter. These plants

Beauty Berry

Butterfly Bush

provide an important food supply for birds during winter, as well as a safe refuge to nest and protection from predators.

Crimson bottlebrush

(*Callistemon citrinus*)

The aptly named bottlebrush provides the garden with lovely, early summer colour. This plant will thrive best in sunny conditions, in well-drained soil. The cylindrical spikes of red flowers of *Callistemon citrinus* appear on willowy stems in June and July. Even when not flowering, this bottlebrush provides a lot of interest to the garden, with evergreen leaves producing a slightly lemony scent when touched. Grows to approximately 1.5 m high by 1.5 m wide.

Echinacea (Coneflower)

This powerhouse of health can be sown easily from seed. Lovely pinky-purple, daisy-like flowers make echinacea the ideal addition to a wildflower bed or meadow. Plant seeds from March and April for a lovely display of blooms in late summer and autumn. Seeds can be collected in late autumn for a spring sowing. This hardy plant prefers full sun or partial shade and will do well in most soil types, dying back completely for the winter.

Forsythia

This perennial shrub makes the spring garden a much brighter place with its eye-catching yellow flowers that appear before the leaves in early spring. There are many varieties of this hardy shrub to choose from and all of them will do well in most soil types, although they prefer full sun to part shade and moist, well-drained soil. *Forsythias* can grow quite large, so it is a good idea to prune them back after they have finished flowering to stop them growing out of control.

Fountain grass

(*Pennisetum*)

There are numerous varieties of *Pennisetum*, or fountain grass as it is commonly known, that will enhance any garden in the warm weather. A clumping evergreen grass, fountain grass appears like a green sunburst, feathery flowers growing in pale pinks and reds out of the tufting foliage. Grow in full sun to light shade and plant in moist, well-drained soil – although fountain grass will grow in any soil except those that are poorly drained. These beautiful ornamental grasses flower in the summer months and should be pruned back, or separated, in the spring.

Fuchsia

One of the unique features of the hedgerows in the west and south-west of Ireland is the fuchsia blossom during the summer. Native to South America, Central America, Mexico

Echinacea

Fuchsia

and Tahiti, *fuchsia* is now naturalized in West Cork and other parts of Ireland. It is *Fuchsia magellanica* and its varieties that grow wild in Ireland. These deciduous plants can grow to 3 m in height, though I would recommend keeping them to 1–1.5 m for a more compact plant. To me, the flower of the fuchsia is one of the real wonders of nature, each petal so beautifully crafted and presented, each flower a work of art in itself. There are dozens, if not hundreds, of varieties, mostly not frost hardy and grown as summer-flowering pot plants.

Hydrangea

This charming, deciduous, summer-flowering shrub comes in many varieties, producing pink, blue-purple and white flowers in either a lacecap or mophead form. All varieties of hydrangea prefer a damp, moist soil and semi-shade. They grow to a height and spread of 1.5–2 m and need to be pruned back in February/March to maintain health. One of the loveliest for any garden is *Hydrangea arborescens* 'Annabelle', which has large, smooth, white flowers and will do well in a shady area of your garden.

Lavender

(*Lavandula angustifolia* 'Hidcote') Lavander is an aromatic plant that produces scented blue flowers from May to August. 'Hidcote' is a good compact variety, ideal for use as a hedge or on its own. This lavender grows to 40 cm in height and 30 cm wide and is suitable for planting in a warm, well-drained position. All parts of the plant can be harvested for their herbal properties. Similar to the *hebes*, lavender will become 'woody' if not pruned. I recommend cutting back the dead flower stems and a little of the foliage after flowering (around October) and cutting back again by about 20 per cent in March to keep the plant compact. If left to get 'woody', it cannot be cut back hard, as it will just curl up and die.

Leucothoe

The genus *Leucothoe* is made up pre-dominately of evergreen species with some semi-evergreen and deciduous species. It is an ideal plant for ground cover and mass plantings and perfect for a sunny or semi-shaded spot in your garden. Use the beautifully coloured leaves to cover the base of other plants or just grow them for use in bouquets. There are many varieties of *Leucothoe* that produce foliage ranging from deep purples to variegated greens and yellows. The attractive clusters of creamy white, scented flowers are a lovely feature in any garden. Two varieties to try are *Leucothoe fontanesiana* 'Scarletta', growing only to about 50 cm with fantastic foliage, and *Leucothoe fontanesiana* 'Rainbow',

Hydrangea

French Lavender

which grows to about 1 m and is must for the garden in autumn and winter because of its colourful dark green leaves, mottled with cream and pink.

Mock orange blossom (*Philadelphus*)
This tall, deciduous shrub produces lovely strongly scented, white flowers during the summer months. Growing to approximately 3 m high by 3 m wide, the mock orange blossom thrives in moist, well-drained soil and in full sunlight. This plant, with its 5 cm flowers, is a must for lovers of fragrant gardens.

Pineapple lily (*Eucomis*)
Eucomis, or the Pineapple lily, is a member of the hyacinth family, which is generally grown from bulbs. Plants are quite tender and therefore do best in a sheltered spot where they get full sun. The flowering period is late summer to mid-autumn, when it is important to keep them well watered. They are often grown in pots in sheltered areas and then placed, or planted out, in the warm summer months. Try *Eucomis vandermerwei* 'Octopus' in a gravel bed; its lovely dark foliage showing up dramatically against the coloured gravel.

Purple smoke bush
(*Cotinus coggygria* 'Royal Purple')
The purple smoke bush is famed for its beautiful deep purple foliage. Plant in sunny conditions in well-drained soil and watch as this wonder of the garden produces smoky pink flowers through the summer months, creating the illusion that the plant is covered in a pink smoke. This deciduous shrub is hardy and can provide years of interest to your garden, changing colours with the seasons and growing to 3 m in height if desired.

St John's wort (*Hypericum* 'Hidcote')
An evergreen shrub, St John's wort is hardy and relatively easy to grow. The golden yellow flowers of *Hypericum* 'Hidcote', which are produced from May to October, are the largest to be produced by any *Hypericum*, growing to about 5 cm across. They prefer full sun or partial shade and will tolerate hard pruning if they outgrow their desired space. Grow in moist, well-drained soil.

Spiraea japonica 'Firelight'
Growing to approximately 80 cm high, this attractive shrub is another one for the butterflies. It produces orange spring growth that gives way to fiery red autumn colour. Deep pink/red flowers arrive in the summer, covering the plant. This variety does not revert to green like 'Goldflame'. If planted in full sun/semi-shade, the *Spiraea* will do well in most soils.

Star magnolia (*Magnolia stellata*)
Star magnolia is, in fact, the star of

Magnolia

many gardens. Its beautiful white, scented flowers open before the leaves appear, generally from March to April. When mature, this majestic bush grows to 2–3 m, making it an ideal choice for a small garden. Plant in part shade to full sun and in well-drained soil. This plant prefers an acidic soil but can tolerate small amounts of lime; it is fairly hardy but the buds can be damaged by frost, so it is important to ensure that the plant gets some sun each day.

Chapter 5

Begonia tuberosa

One of the finest of the summer flowering plants, *begonias* thrive in a range of light, from full sun to shade. Dark, fleshy leaves are produced from March onwards and from May to September huge flowers are produced in pink, orange, red, peach, white and yellow. They like rich, loose and fertile soil, which drains well. Water thoroughly, then allow the soil to dry before the next watering. To keep them looking lovely all season, remove dead flowers, leaves and stems.

Cabbage palm (*Cordyline australis*)

The cabbage palm comes from 'down under' to add a touch of the exotic to our gardens. This spiky plant, with its long thin, arching leaves, provides a perfect feature plant for any sunny to part shade area of the garden. Although *C. australis* is hardy, the varieties 'Torbay Dazzler' and 'Torbay Red' need to be protected from severe frosts, so it is best either to plant them in a container or ensure that they are in a sheltered hot spot in your garden. Leaves should be covered in a particularly cold winter.

Cyclamen

A good choice for any garden, the hardy *cyclamen* will bloom for up to nine months of the year. It thrives in part to full shade and therefore does well around the base of other feature plants and in containers. *Cyclamens* come in a variety of colours, from white to deep red, and for best results are grown in soil rich in organic matter. To prevent the tubers from drying out in the summer or winter months, mulch with leaf mould. *Cyclamen hederifolium* unfurls its flowers on coil-like stems, which look like springs in the autumn and winter, and *Cyclamen coum* is a great variety for spring flowering. All *cyclamens* have beautifully marbled leaves.

Gladiolus

If you want your own personal florist in your back garden, then planting *gladioli* is a great idea. These beautiful flowering corms come in all the colours of the rainbow and will provide bright, colourful interest to the sunny

Cyclamen

spots in your garden throughout the summer months. Plant the corms (bulb-like structures) in May in loose, well-drained soil and spaced approximately 16 cm apart; stake at the time of planting. Corms can be purchased from any garden centre and come with detailed instructions on how to plant and overwinter.

Heather

A beautiful flowering plant that is easy to maintain, heather will give your garden colour in the greyest months of the year. In fact, you can have a heather in flower every month of the year if you choose the right varieties. *Erica carnea* (Alpine heath) and *Erica darleyensis* (Darley Dale heath) flower in winter and spring and are suited to all soil types. *Erica cinerea* (bell heather) will flower in late spring and summer and needs an acidic soil, while *Erica vagans* (Cornish heath) will grow in most soils, flowering in late summer and autumn. *Daboecia*, the Irish bell heather, is another species that needs an acidic soil and flowers in spring and again in autumn. *Calluna vulgaris* (Scots heather) will flower into autumn and also needs an acidic soil.

Lily

Lilies are one of the best additions to any garden. They are easy to grow and come in beautiful colours and textures to create interest in any sunny spot

that has rich, well-drained soil. If you plant a mixture of early, mid and late flowering varieties, then you can guarantee flowers from June to September. Lilies are usually grown from bulbs planted in early spring or autumn. Make sure to select good firm bulbs and plant them immediately after purchase. Position each bulb slightly on its side, with some grit below it to prevent water collecting around the bulb. Watering the base of the lily rather than the petals and leaves will help to reduce any threat of disease, but watch out for rabbits and slugs, which like to nibble on the emerging plant. Types to look out for are the Asiatic lilies and the Oriental lilies, which are strongly scented, and the tiger lilies.

New Zealand flax (*Phormium*)

Whichever variety of *Phormium* you choose for your garden will be a winning feature. Large and often colourful, spiky plants, they work well in containers as well as in the ground. Preferring full sun or partial shade, these stunning evergreens have tough, sword-like leaves that shoot up from the base of the plant. Look for different varieties in bronze, pinks, silvers and reds. Plant in rich, moist soil, and check before purchase that the variety you have chosen is correct for your space, as heights can vary, from *Phormium* 'Duet' which grows to

Heather

Lily

Fuchsia

Index

Snowdrop